Oklahoma Proud!

![cattle grazing in field with mountains in background]

A Centennial Book of Poems
by
Eddie D. Wilcoxen

CTK PUBLISHING

Oklahoma Proud!

Copyright © 2007 by Eddie D. Wilcoxen

All rights reserved. Except for brief passages quoted in a newspaper, magazine, radio or television review, no part of this book may be reproduced in any form or by any means, electronic or mechanical, including photocopying and recording, or by any information storage and retrieval system, without permission in writing from CTK Publishing, or the author Eddie D. Wilcoxen at CTK Publishing, 801 North Main St., Altus, Oklahoma 73521 or www.Eddiestuff.com

Cover Credits:

Longhorns in Wichita Mountains Wildlife Refuge
Photo by Eddie D. Wilcoxen (see more at Eddiestuff.com)

Sunset at Quartz Mountain
Photo by Carolyn Shumaker

Audio Information:
Enjoy the special audio reading of selected passages by Eddie D. Wilcoxen

**Visit www.Eddiestuff.com
for information on other books and projects.**

Please write to Eddie Wilcoxen with comments or to schedule a reading:
712 East Walker Street
Altus, Ok 73521
phone 580-471-9733
email: wilcoxens@sbcglobal.net

LIBRARY OF CONGRESS CATALOGING-IN-PUBLICATION DATA

ISBN 978-0-6151-4312-5

CTK PUBLISHING

**PRINTED IN THE UNITED STATES OF AMERICA
FIRST EDITION**

OKLAHOMA PROUD! CONTENTS

Acknowledgements 7	Red River Sunset 48
Introduction 8	Cheshire Moon 49
Rhyming the Western Sky 11	Great Western Trail 51
Route 66 12	Little Sahara 53
Thanks Theodore 14	Quiet Cove 54
Hugo Bluegrass 16	Fall Show 55
Redbud 17	Bill Pickett 56
Oil! 18	Spring Rain 57
Price Falls 20	Cattle Drive 58
Mistletoe 22	Ladder of Rivers 59
Black Mesa 23	Oklahoma Proud! 59
Stand Waite 24	Southwest Oklahoma 60
Lights in the Valley Tonight ... 25	Bat Cave 60
Little Prairie Home 26	Gusher! 61
Buckskin Joe 28	Seven Hells 62
Beaver's Bend 30	King Cotton 65
Winter 31	Oklahoma Lullaby 67
Jumping the Cimarron 32	Turner Falls 68
Sooner, Not Later 33	The '89ers 69
Goodbye to the Cowboy 35	Eagle Watch 70
Belle Starr 36	Quartz Mountains 71
Guthrie 37	Jim Thorpe 72
Heavener Runestone 38	Pond Song 73
Geronimo 39	Forest Magic 74
Oklahoma Home 40	Scissortail 75
Rattlesnakes 41	The Three Guardsmen 76
Thunderstorm 42	The Hanging Judge 77
Oklahoma Difference 44	Coming Home 78
Coyotes 45	Brahma Lesson 79
Fox 45	The Wichitas 80
Will Rogers 46	Sequoyah 82
Wiley Post 47	Jester's Cave 83

OKLAHOMA PROUD! CONTENTS (continued)

Cutthroat Gap 84	Spaceport 95
Spanish Silver 85	Stripers!.................................... 96
Quanah Parker.....................87	Remington Park 97
Bricktown.............................88	Buffaloes Return 98
State Fair 89	Medicine Park 99
Sunset of the West 90	Death Song............................. 100
Old Timers 91	Kill the Mountain 101
Tulsa 91	Rollin' Home........................... 102
Oklahoma Wildflowers.......92	So Glad I'm Home.................. 103
Crosstimbers.......................93	Oklahoma City Memorial 104
Happy Birthday, Okalahoma! ...94	Home 105
Freedom, Oklahoma 94	Index.. 107
Space Shuttle 95	

Acknowledgements

This book would have been far less without the terrific assistance of the loyal listeners of the KWHW **MORNING SHOW** who keep me company every day starting at 5 am.

A sincere thank you to each of you for your support, suggestions, and for the invaluable contribution of some wonderful photographs!

I am privileged to share with you the works of some very talented Oklahoma photographers whose photos I have enjoyed, and I am thrilled that they have allowed me to include them in this Centennial Book of Poems! I extend my heartfelt appreciation for sharing your talented work with all of us to my friends and photographic artists: Tyrone Penick, Barbara Blocker, Cheri Maloney, Mary Kromer, Paul Long, Paul McEndree, Scott Young, Nelda Cable, Kristin Kelly, and Melissa Burns.

The Museum of the Western Prairie in Altus, Ok is a great research source, with an amazing collection of historic photographs from the early settlement of this area. A special thank you to Bart McClenny and everybody there for their assistance and indulgence.

Some of the selections included in "Oklahoma Proud!" are from my Reflections series, some from the Songbook series, and still others will be found in the forthcoming, "Train of Thought!" Most, however, are original to this book. I hope you enjoy them, and thanks again to everyone who helped!

………..Eddie D. Wilcoxen

Introduction

"Oklahoma, where the wind comes sweeping down the plain...." It just sounds poetic! For about thirty years now, southwest Oklahoma has been my home. They say there's no believer like a convert, and I am always ready to sing Oklahoma's praises!

I am originally from Kansas, but lived all over the United States before I chose to settle here. My wife Joan came from Long Island, New York to visit her family in Oklahoma each summer for ten years before she decided to move here, where we eventually met. The wonderful solid values and warm and friendly culture of Oklahoma made us each feel at home, so we embraced this as our permanent home together.

For all these thirty years, whenever we get the chance, we have been exploring the sights of Oklahoma, from Black Mesa in the far west panhandle to Beaver's Bend in the southeast corner and many parts between. This year, with all the talk of the 2007 statehood centennial, I realized that this was the perfect time for a project I had long been planning— a book of poems about the events, the people, the places, and the feel of Oklahoma!

If you live here, I hope it strikes a chord of truth, and if you don't, I hope it makes you want to visit.

Come see us and enjoy the sights, but be forewarned! I came here to visit for a few days, and stayed for thirty years!

………..Eddie D. Wilcoxen

Oklahoma Proud!

A Centennial Book of Poems

Western Oklahoma — Photo by Mary Kromer

RHYMING THE WESTERN SKY

The mountain peaks punctuate the sweeping prairie reach,
and all around the wondrous song of coyotes as they preach!

And high above, an azure sky stretches out for miles,
while billowing white thunderheads roll on free and wild!

It's the sky out in the West! It's where I live today,
and as I watch the sun go down, I can't believe I went away!

Purple paints the western sky, and the orange tint covers all;
from blue, to purple, to orange, down to that red, red sinking ball.

The sun sits on the horizon, and the beauty of its rhyme
stirs something deep within my soul, time, after time, after time.

And as the sky turns darker, and stars come out to play,
the last dim rays of the sun fade out and gently go away,

leaving twilight's illusions, shadows on shadows and light,
dim to the eye that is waiting for the moon to enter the night.

And as on a stage for an actor, the setting is perfect and more,
as the moon makes its entrance like a starlet of Hollywood lore!

Full blown and radiant, with bright reflected light,
the moon casts down its magic on this soft enchanted night.

And as the night birds start their calling, joining the coyotes din,
there can be no finer place on earth, than the Western Rhyme I'm in!

ROUTE 66

From North to South and to the West it sweeps -
it's called the Mother Road.
It carries a nation's priceless human wealth -
they are the mother lode!

There is this place called America,
where everyone can stand,
a place where families live in peace,
working hand in hand.

But somehow it got lost
in the wind and dust and drought.
Still they're out there searching,
pouring from the South,

leaving the land that's forsaken them -
that has stolen all they own -
and in dying scorn it blows away,
and last it takes their homes.

They are the modern Jews,
headed out of Egypt to the promised land.
There is a path out of this wilderness,
this desolate, dry land -

Route 66! Gateway to the West!
It carries all their dreams:
their hopes for a place to live and work,
for home, and all it means.

Westward they pour, Okies on the move,
escaping from the dust!
A common goal, a single path,
"California or we bust! "

A million dreams went down Route 66,
and some were left to die,
a million hopes and plans,
in cars, and trucks, and buses loaded high!

Route 66! Gateway to a better life!
They traveled it with faith;
with prayers and determination,
they chase the slippery wraith!

We know some found that better life,
some only the bitter end of road,
where the heartaches and disappointments
piled so high they couldn't tote the load.

Route 66! The stuff of legends -
much bigger than is real!
It's a piece of America,
a past that time can't steal.

But the Mother Road is gone now,
or only bits remain.
And like the human tide that rolled this way,
it won't be back again.

Still, the ghosts of those who traveled
down this lost highway
speak to us of the places
and the time of their great getaway.

When this was **the** road - the road to paradise!
And Route 66 will never die -
it's the stuff of legends
because of all their sacrifice!

Route 66! It's the Grapes of Wrath, and TV shows,
and western songs, and motels by the score!
It is a thousand cities split by a road -
but joined by the motor's roar!

THANKS, THEODORE!

Theodore was an eastern chap,
but he loved these western lands,
and as President of the U.S.A.
for the West he took a stand.

He created national parks,
and national forests, too;
he worked to preserve their beauty
for the likes of me and you!

Among his many signings
was one of Oklahoma's own:
The Wichita Mountain Wildlife Refuge,
soon to be the buffalo's new home.

It was the salvation of the longhorn,
and the elk returned as well
to roam these craggy mountains
and to graze the grassy dell.

Thousands of acres were saved
from the threat of cow and plow.
Thanks to Theodore Roosevelt,
we have this jewel now!

So as you drive through its rocky beauty
or hike by pristine lakes,
tip your hat to Theodore!
He helped to make it great!

One of many lakes in the Wichita Wildlife Refuge - Photo by Tyrone Penick

HUGO BLUEGRASS

The music of America,
rings out across the land!
Everywhere around the park,
people sit, and talk, and stand.

And you can hear the ringing banjoes,
the strum of soft guitars,
the murmur of happy people
gathered 'neath the stars.

It's Bluegrass down in Hugo!
And they come from near and far.
They fill up every place in town,
some sleep out in their car.

They share a love of music,
of good friends, and the Lord.
On Sunday in the park, in the dawning morn,
they strike a common chord,

giving thanks for all their blessings
and lifting spirits high!
It's Bluegrass down in Hugo,
a place to be before you die!

REDBUD

In the waning days of winter
across these Oklahoma hills,
purple leaves proclaim
that coming spring will soon be beauty filled.

It's the blooming of the Redbuds,
our Oklahoma tree,
whose colors bright
cheer the hearts of everyone who sees.

After spring has passed
and purple turned to green,
the redbud recedes into the landscape,
seldom to be seen.

But for a short while, the colors blaze
in quite a splendid show,
as the Redbud tree unfolds its leaves
and bids the winter go!

OIL!

The black gold rolled and flowed
from this Oklahoma land!
Oil derricks blocked the sun,
barely room for a man to stand.

Fortunes made and lost, and fortunes made again -
the oil men rolled the dice!
Punch a hole and bust, or punch a hole and gusher;
no matter, they would pay the price!

It was the new frontier of oil and mud,
and rugged roughneck men,
who did the dangerous work by day,
and by night they practiced sin!

They were living for the moment,
going hard and fast.
Making money, spending more -
they knew it couldn't last!

Oklahoma oil! It was pumped to run this land.
Oklahoma oil! That smooth black siren
called to the soul of every eager man!

And it lifted some to greatness,
and fortunes beyond belief!
In the Oklahoma of the rich,
it was not gold, but oil that paved the streets.

Still, after all these years,
the name Oklahoma summons oil,
and images of boomtowns
springing from the soil!

Oklahoma, where that black gold
rolled and flowed,
was the engine of America -
its future bright and bold.

But as quickly as they started
the boom days faded fast.
New fields were found in other places;
it wasn't meant to last.

But for just a while Oklahoma was
the darling of them all -
where that black oil flowed in rivers
and the roughnecks worked and brawled!

Photo Courtesy of the Museum of the Western Prairie—Altus, OK

PRICE FALLS

My old map showed a treasure
hidden in South Oklahoma,
yet clearly marked to see.

It told of a place called Price Falls,
in the Arbuckles,
and that was where I meant to be.

Nearing my destination,
I drove up and down, and back and forth
but not even one sign could I find.

So I pulled into the driveway
of the Odd Fellows Camp nearby
said, "I'm in kind of a bind."

"I'm looking for Price Falls,
I can't find it anywhere.
can you tell me where to look?"

The Odd Fellow man looked stern,
stepped down off the porch,
said, "Son, let me see that book!"

Then he told me Price Falls was private,
and shouldn't be on my map,
but he could see that it was there.

He told me he was going to bend the rules
and gave us directions to Price Falls,
just down the thoroughfare.

So we walked a quiet woodland path
past an old time water wheel.
and on down toward the stream.

Then rounding a bend in the trail,
we just stopped in admiration,
as we entered in a dream!

Price Falls was right there before us -
it was less than ten feet high -
but how those sparkling waters danced!

And all around us emerald green,
the moss was growing thick and rich!
The scene truly did entrance!

You half expected to see fairies
or little woodland sprites
come dancing by.

The trees surround,
the waters sound,
it's nature's lullaby!

Quietly we sat beside the hidden falls;
stayed for an hour or so;
then other duties called.

So, silent and content,
we walked back along the path.
We had been to see Price Falls!

MISTLETOE

Do you know the story of how
the mistletoe came to be Oklahoma's flower?
For mistletoe is a parasite -
seldom compared to the rose's glowing bower!

In 1891, not long after the first run, in Pottawatomie County
a young wife grew sick and died.
Her husband and a neighbor fashioned
a home made coffin for the lamented bride's last ride.

It was a bleak and cold December,
and no flowers could be found.
Nothing green grew anywhere
from frozen, barren ground.

There was nothing to soften the casket's
stark and grim outline but mistletoe.
So from nearby trees they gathered some,
as they trudged through falling snow.

And the neighbor said,
 "Son, you've done her proud - the best that you can do,
and that mistletoe has served us well,
and I'll see it gets it due."

"If I ever have the chance, I'll see it basked in glory."
And at the constitutional convention,
they voted it the Oklahoma flower,
after the man told them this story.

BLACK MESA

In the far western corner of Oklahoma
rises Black Mesa, the highest land in the state.
Too long since I've seen Black Mesa -
got to get back to that place.

It's a sky as wide as all the world,
and a greeting warm as cozy fire.
It's an old time feeling in an ancient land -
flat top mesas rising higher!

Here the cattle graze,
amidst the sleepy days and gentle ways.
Here the cactus bloom, and
the Cimarron meanders through the far blue haze.

Mesquite lands still speak
of an older people's path
to the Rockies, and of the wandering buffalo.

Let's climb the Black Mesa,
stand upon the rocky top
and watch the world turn down below!

The mesas rise up in the west,
and this land just reaches on and on.
It's a rugged place of sweeping beauty,
a glimpse of days bygone!

Black Mesa - Photo by Cheri Maloney

STAND WAITE

Stand Waite was a General,
raised in the Cherokee way.
He fought with the Confederacy, for Indian Independence,
convinced a win would save the day!

Oklahoma's Stand Waite was the last Confederate,
the last to lay down arms.
He was a Brigadier General,
leader of the famous Cherokee Braves,
straight from the Honey Creek farm.

He led his Rebel Raiders to victory many times,
and at the second Cabin Creek,
they took millions in supplies!

He captured the steamship J.R. Williams,
led his troopers well.
But eventually the cause was lost -
the North had rung its knell!

So in June of 1865,
Stand Waite surrendered up his sword.
He knew his dream of Indian independence
was gone forever more.

So Stand Waite went home to Honey Creek
to live his last years out.
But he leaves behind his tales and songs
of bravery, that linger in the South!

LIGHTS IN THE VALLEY TONIGHT

I'm standing here at the top of the hill,
I've been out walking alone.
Sometimes I need to get away;
it's a feeling down deep in my bones.

Usually I'm pretty happy and content,
that's the way I shape it!
But lately I've been feeling melancholy,
and I just can't fake it.

So I'm out walking, and thinking,
and watching the world,
and I know perspective will come.
Somehow I'll regain my center
so my life's race I can run!

I've got some friends who are in trouble,
going through really rough times.
And I can't shake this sadness.
It mirrors me just like a mime.

I feel the burden of grief,
and carry with me its weight,
all the way to the top of the hill,
then into the valley I gaze.

And the just setting sun
is casting a glow,
as I look with wonder
into the valley below!

The world is deep purple and pink,
and there are points of light in the darkness.
Shining bright beacons of light,
they contrast with all of the starkness.

And suddenly, the weight is gone!
My heart is new and light!
It will be all right I know,
there are lights in the valley tonight!

Old Homestead - Photo by Paul Long

LITTLE PRAIRIE HOME

Where is the man who built me? Who labored day and night?
Long it's been since he left here, with his children and his wife.

I miss their laughter in the hall, the squeal of children's play;
no more the light of kerosene lamp at the darkened end of day.

I hear no quiet bedtime prayers, no whispered secrets sweet.
Boarded and shuttered and left alone, no one do I meet.

Occasionally through the passing years, as I fall into disrepair,
someone will come and wander here, wondering who it was lived here?

If only they could hear me! What a tale I'd tell -
of love and sorrow, pleasure and pain, of heaven and of hell!

I've seen the bitter struggles, seen tears of joy and pain.
I've heard the sounds of nighttime love, and anguished cries for rain!

Through these broken empty panes, hungry eyes have stared a thousand times,
wondering about the world beyond this quiet country lane,
past all this work and country grime.

I know it wasn't easy, but the children always ate,
and once I had new paint, a picket fence, and wooden garden gate.

Through the years, I've lost some shingles, the porch is torn askew.
Nearby, the well is dry, the windmill too ramshackle to ever turn anew.

The swallows nest up in my eaves, the rabbits in the yard.
The trees they planted long ago still linger, but life for them is hard.

The tumbleweeds roll by my door, the coyote howls nearby
and I am empty and alone, as through me night winds sigh.

My time came and went so quickly - happy family here- then gone to flight.
Little time remains for me, but while I stand,
perhaps someone will see, and then will write!

Will write about the way I sheltered them, kept them safe and warm.
Will tell of my noble efforts to shield them from life's storms!

Perhaps someone will tell of my service - loyal through and through -
when this country was first settled and homes were far and few!

BUCKSKIN JOE

Buckskin Joe was a booster,
talked of Oklahoma land.
Said, "This is the place for you, boys,
more prosperity than anyone can stand!"

"There is timber for the taking,
land for farming, too.
The climate there is mild,
your troubles will be few!"

Well, we told you he was a booster,
and Buckskin Joe was smooth.
It wasn't long before from Fort Worth
two hundred were ready for the move.

They came north to Old Greer County, Texas,
and started them a town,
just west of the Red River's North Fork.
They named it Navajoe, and proclaimed it the finest all around!

These settlers came to Oklahoma
to make themselves a home,
and through blizzards, droughts, and hard times,
they built their houses of dirt, and wood, and stone.

And here they raised their families,
who in turn raised theirs,
and the passing of the years brought better times,
and relief from pressing cares.

So let's tip our hat to old Buckskin Joe
who founded Navajoe,
one of the biggest towns in Oklahoma,
it was also first to go.

When the railroad came in to the south,
they platted in the town of Headrick,
and soon Navajoe was gone, moved to the railroad.
The people made their pick!

Today in Navajoe there is no town,
just the echo of a far off train.
The hotel and the racetrack gone,
only the graveyard still remains.

The townsfolk have all left us,
the Kiowa and Comanche too.
But once, Navajoe was a bustling town
when Buckskin Joe came through!

BEAVER'S BEND

The diamond dew is shining in the morning sun,
and the mist is rising on the water.

Set against the wooded mountain backdrop,
Beaver's Bend is home to the wandering forest daughter!

In early morning quiet, she sprinkles out her blessing,
then rushes away to greet her Oklahoma father.

Together, through magic lands, where time is forgotten,
they dance to a woodland tune, far from civilization's fodder!

Photo by Mary Kromer

<u>WINTER</u>

Bare limbs, sparse light,
winter austerity -
contrasting in my mind
with summer's shining plenty.

The sun beats coldly
in a world of white,
and the shadows shrink away
giving up the fight.

Bundled bodies hurry by,
looking for some shelter -
a place away from the biting wind
that blows around us helter skelter!

JUMPING THE CIMARRON

I've seen the Cimarron a half-mile wide
at its conjunction with the Arkansas.
But I've jumped across the Cimarron
and not even wet my feet, down there in the draw!

That was out in the far west reaches
of where the river runs,
before it fills with water spilled
from the land through which it comes.

But we must remember the Cimarron
is called the "river that runs dry."
For many miles in the heat of summer
no water flows on by.

It just puddles here and there -
few signs of glories yet to come,
out in far west Oklahoma,
early on the Cimarron!

SOONER NOT LATER

There were those so eager to settle in this land
that they just couldn't wait.
They came here a little early,
gave their name to this whole state.

They were called the Sooners,
and they were eager for to work,
ready to start anew - to dig in
and their duty never shirk.

So when the gunshot sounded
and the race for land began,
the Sooners were already on the scene,
the situation well in hand.

Some would call it cheating,
but to the victor go the spoils,
and soon that would be born out dramatic
with Oklahoma oil!

So Oklahoma is the land of the Sooners,
the land of quick new starts,
a place for those who want to work and play
and follow imagination's spark.

But you'd better do it sooner,
and you'd better never wait,
or someone else will do it first!
We're the Sooner State!

Near Humphreys, OK - Photo by Kristin Kelly

GOODBYE TO THE COWBOY

As the blood red sun settles in the west,
one lone horseman slowly rides away.
He's leaving the land he helped to win;
he's lived well past his day!

He remembers this land before the fences,
this country without the towns;
when a day's ride to anywhere
brought only nature's sounds.

He recalls the hardships of the trail;
the dust, the cold, the wind.
And he knows that if youth's vigor could be restored
he'd do it all again!

But the West has kept on changing,
filled with people, cut by roads.
Where an old cowboy can find some peace,
heaven only knows!

So he's saddled up his faithful friend,
and set out for a ride.
It's his last one he figures,
and quietly he sighs.

"It's been one hell of a run;
I wouldn't trade it for anything.
So, Adios, Goodbye, I'll see you on the other side,
riding high on angel wings!"

BELLE STARR

Belle Starr was a Bandit Queen, made herself a name.
Moved back up from Dallas, brought trouble as she came!

She was famous for her flamboyant ways; she traveled with panache -
with Stetson hat and ostrich plume,
and twin pearl handled pistols she would flash!

Rustling, bootlegging, stealing horses too -
Belle was game for anything if it paid the money due!

She spent a year in Fort Smith prison, beat all you ever saw.
The day they let her out, she said, "I'm a friend to all outlaws!"

But Belle's life was a short one, shot down at 41.
Riding home to Eufaula, she was cut down by a gun.

They never found who did it, some said they never tried,
but her daughter Pearl said, "Let it go, there's no need to cry."

She wrote for Belle this epitaph, engraved it on her stone.
These are the departing thoughts about Belle Starr, her last and final tome:

> **"Shed not for her a bitter tear,**
> **nor give the heart to vain regret;**
> **tis but the casket that lies here,**
> **the gem that filled it sparkles yet!"**

GUTHRIE

Among the towns here in the West, Guthrie is most unique.
It's the perfect place to go if Oklahoma flavor's what you seek!

Settled on that first day of the Oklahoma Run,
Guthrie was the Territorial Capitol, its fortune seemed then won.

But with the approach of statehood, a battle soon ensued
between Guthrie and Oklahoma City. When it ended the capitol had moved!

Guthrie went from booming town to almost empty over night.
Many fortunes were lost there, it seemed a lonely plight.

But in the end it was a blessing, not a curse,
because it was not the end of Guthrie, just the changing of the verse.

For more than fifty years, Guthrie sat unchanged,
while to the south in Oklahoma City, great deeds were under way.

And when the state awakened to its history and its pride,
it turned its glance to Guthrie and could not believe its eyes!

Here stood a vision of a glorious past, waiting there for us!
Yes, it had become ramshackle, but there was beauty in that dust!

So with renewed pride the Guthrie folk set out to start again.
With love and sweat they restored their town to what it once had been!

There's just no place like it; the history, the architecture, the tales;
like the talk of Tom Mix, the movie star, the stories of those who won or failed.

It's a living, breathing time capsule, a glimpse into the past!
So welcome to old Guthrie, a window into Oklahoma's past
that is truly meant to last!

HEAVENER RUNESTONE

Long ago, across this land the mighty Viking strode!
The proof is near Heavener, Oklahoma, just east of the road.

Up in a hidden valley is the Heavener Runestone,
a relic of the Vikings when they called this valley home.

The markings are clear to see, though fading with the years,
and the proof is clearly demonstrated, despite scholastic jeers.

Not far from the Runestone, a smaller two were found,
and the indications are they marked the Viking boundary ground.

They showed the area ruled by an ancient Viking King,
who had traveled up the river, and stopped at the nearby stream.

Can you imagine the journey these Norsemen must have made -
to travel all the way to Oklahoma - across the bounding waves,

and then around the shoreline of America, and out into the Gulf
and up the Mississippi, like some adventure of Beowulf?

Did they ever make it home to tell their tales of travel?
Or are their bones in some hidden place this mystery to unravel?

We will probably never know; the answers won't be found;
but its pretty certain, that at one time in Oklahoma,
the Vikings were around!

Geronimo - Photo Courtesy of the Museum of the Western Prairie, Altus, OK

GERONIMO

GERONIMO, proud Apache chief,
GERONIMO, wild spirit leap,
GERONIMO, man of legend,
GERONIMO, his deeds transcend!

GERONIMO, prisoner of war,
GERONIMO, he paced the floor,
GERONIMO, in old Fort Sill,
GERONIMO, his spirit lingers still!

GERONIMO, a famous cry,
GERONIMO WILL NEVER DIE!

OKLAHOMA HOME

I came to Oklahoma, a young man bound to roam.
I had tried most everywhere; I had those restless bones!

On my way to Colorado, I stopped here for a while
to visit with my brother Lee, and share with him a smile.

I was only going to stay for a few days at the most,
but Lee and Oklahoma were such gracious hosts,

that thirty years have come and gone, and still I linger here,
with roots too deep to leave, and many friends so dear.

I've lived here longer than anywhere. I consider it my home.
And I'm proud to be an Okie, so never more I'll roam!

RATTLESNAKES

Ra-Ra-Ra-Rattlesnakes! The very name strikes fear!
Ra-Ra-Ra-Rattlesnakes! The bane of the pioneer!

In Oklahoma, these vipers of the rocks and hills winter underground.
In dens of hundreds, they hibernate, waiting for spring to come around.

Then they leave their cold weather refuge and slither off to hunt,
and many a field mouse becomes a rattler's lunch!

Men from towns like Mangum and Waurika scour the hills and fields,
and gather rattlesnakes with the forked sticks they wield.

They throw them in a sack, bring them down to town, and invite the world!
It's an occasion for a festival, and thousands come to see the rattlers curled!

They watch the handlers in the pit, they "ooh" and "ahh" and squeal.
They dine on fried rattlesnake, a "tastes like chicken" meal!

There'll be a flea market and a carnival, and people everywhere,
and meanwhile back in the rock outcrops the rattlesnakes don't care.

They soak up the gathering heat, and look for things to eat,
as they follow the ancient rhythm of nature's steady beat.

Rattlesnakes roam these hills, not a thing to revile and fear,
but an amazing creature to be admired and studied, and honored once a year!

Lightning North of Altus - Photo by Scott Young

THUNDERSTORM

The Oklahoma sky rolls on,
unbroken blue and white.
The clouds are gathering,
gentle ripples join
and climb to dismaying heights.

Billows and pillars, and swirling shapes
foretell a weather change,
as far away sheet lightning flashes
its warning across the sweeping plains.

And high overhead as the storm approaches,
lightning illuminates the clouds,
while from far away and seconds late
the rolling sounds of thunder echo right out loud.

We're here and ready for the show -
a Great Plains Thunderstorm!
If you've never been in one,
you had better be forewarned!

As the storm lumbers nearer,
the lightning can be seen, leaping cloud to cloud,
like some giant's game of catch;
and the sound is growing loud!

Suddenly the chains of fire
link the heavens and the earth!
You can hear the air sizzle
as the lightning comes to work!

We're surrounded by the sound
of the deep, deep thunder's rumble,
and the evening sits suspended
in this eerie spell it's under.

All nature holds its breath in silence,
except for distant sounds of baying.
Then suddenly the rains pour forth,
as if afraid to stay above,
where the angry Gods are playing!

God Bless America! - Photo by Tyrone Penick

THE OKLAHOMA DIFFERENCE

There's an Oklahoma difference - you can feel it in the air!
You know this is the place - great deeds can happen here!

It's a place that real and true, like the cowboy on the range,
and it carries optimism upon the winds of change!

Anchored solid to the past with an eye on what's to be,
Oklahoma welcomes you. Come join us and you'll see!

You'll find friendly, hard working people; out to do their best,
who with a spirit strong, will help you find your home here in the West!

The Frontier Lake State welcomes you, to hills and rocks and more.
It's here the buffalo still roam, with longhorn and elk; and mighty eagles soar.

And amidst the rugged grandeur a common note is heard -
how you have found a place where a man will keep his word,

where there's a real concern for neighbors, a ready helping hand.
It's a great place for any American to come and proudly stand!

COYOTES

Their piercing lonely howls echo in the night,
an eerie, "yip, yip" of falsetto voices soaring!

It's a coyote pack, sounding out the ancient call,
and it will last into the morning.

A cunning, clever hunter, devoted family man,
for time untold they've hunted across this prairie land,

providing for their youngsters, teaching them the coyote ways,
so they in turn can stand high on a moonlit hill,

and turning eyes to twinkling stars and racing clouds,
lift up their lonely cry, their chant of freedom,
to the darkened sky, and sing their prairie song aloud!

Photo by Paul McEndree

FOX

The quick red fox jumped up on a log
and puppy style he posed like a real hot dog,
before mother yipped, and said, "Come here",
and quick is right! He disappeared!

WILL ROGERS

Will Rogers was most beloved
of all in this great land.
And he was proud to be an Indian,
and of his Oklahoma stand.

He grew up near Oolagah,
east of Tulsa town.
He loved the land and people
and he would have stayed around,

but he had some skill as a cowboy.
A mighty rope he twirled;
he signed on with the 101,
and around the world he toured!

As time went by, at interviews,
Will became the star;
everyone loved to hear him talk,
they came from near and far!

And they began to call him a philosopher,
but Will said it was just common sense,
with a healthy portion of gentle wit,
and homespun humor in the mix.

Will Rogers made movies,
he hobnobbed with the great!
But he never forgot his raisin',
or this Oklahoma state.

And when Will Rogers plane went down in 1935,
the nation was in shock!
They couldn't believe that Will was gone,
that no more they'd hear him talk.

In Claremore, Oklahoma,
you'll find his final resting place.
There's a museum to honor him,
and time to remember Will's smiling, friendly face!

WILEY POST

Wiley Post was an aviation giant;
across these skies he flew;
and the air is filled with planes today
because men like Wiley knew.

They knew the future when they met it,
got right up face to face.
Risking death, they took to wing
and filled the heavens' space!

They went further, longer, faster,
than man had ever gone,
and though Wiley Post is departed now,
his descendants carry on.

Not those born of blood and bone,
but those of the same mind,
who said, "Let's take to the sky
and see what we can find!"

Point Barrow Alaska,
is where old Wiley fell,
acting as a pilot for a man
that we all know so well.

He was another Oklahoman,
Will Rogers was his name,
and though he and Wiley died that day,
they left us ever changed.

Wiley Post loved to fly,
he loved to soar aloft!
He's a legend of the sky, boys,
to him our hats we doff!

Photo by Mary Kromer

RED RIVER SUNSET

From the hilltop I look out across the Red River Valley.

The sun is just going down, setting in a sky both wild and free.

The land is dark, and cut by a golden ribbon of water,
winding as far as the eye can see.

While just above the horizon's glow,
 pink streaks of clouds signal the end of day.

This neon brightness presages the starlight that soon will come to play.
Immersed in this beauty I sit, at the end of dying day.

CHESHIRE MOON

Tonight the crescent moon lay sideways in the sky,
like a silver Cheshire smile.

And as all the stars came out to play,
the world hung suspended for a while!

The shadows danced around, like drunken Elvin sprites,
intoxicated with the dreamy glow of the shimmering golden light.

It was a night of mystery, it was a night of magic,
yet tinged with the mist of ancient feuds, a feeling of the tragic.

Once long ago, the moon hung thus in a long forgotten sky,
and in a land far, far away, the night was passing by.

It was a night, just like tonight, and the moonlight lit the miles,
and the countryside lay captured by a silver Cheshire smile!

Crossing The Red Statue and Jackson County Courthouse - Photo by Eddie Wilcoxen

Where I grew up in Kansas, it was very close to the end of the **GREAT WESTERN CATTLE TRAIL.** *Over this trail millions of longhorns traveled to the railhead in Dodge City.*

Now I live in Oklahoma, very close to where the Great Western Trail enters Oklahoma at it's southern border. The herds forded the Red River near Doan's Crossing, just a few miles south of my home in Altus, and every year there is still a trail ride from Altus to the crossing to commemorate the time of the Great Western Trail.

I've often joked that since the Colorado and the Chisum Trails and many others have their own songs, the Great Western was being slighted, so I hear this poem with a melody. (Jack of Diamonds, Jack of Diamonds..........)

--------------*Eddie D. Wilcoxen*

THE GREAT WESTERN TRAIL

Great Western, Great Western, the Great Western Trail,
blazed by cattle and cowboys o'er hill and through dale.

Great Western, Great Western, we're rarin' to go!
Gathered horns from the breaks and branded them so
up the long trail to Kansas our own cattle we'll know!

Great Western, Great Western, we're all gonna ride,
under skies like an ocean through lands free and wide.

In Texas the cattle live long-horned and free.
They're not ready to follow - bolt each chance they see!
But at last they're a herd and we're ready to leave,
to fight the Great Western with its tricks up its sleeve.

We'll battle the country, the heat, wind and hail,
and ride hell-bent for leather down the Great Western Trail!

We go from Texas to Kansas, through the Indian Lands,
where the last roaming tribes still travel in bands.
Where the grass grows as tall as the buffalo's hump,
the Great Western rolls on - valley, river, and bump.

For eight hundred or more miles, driving ten thousand hoofs,
we're crossing the rivers and cussin' the cook!
Through the days and the weeks of heat and long hours,
some cowboys stay sunny while others just glower!

We cross the Red River at Doan's, it's a breeze,
nice and slow go the cattle, and swim it with ease.
But some ain't so lucky, caught the Red at its flood!
Still the bosses smelled money and risked the wild mud!

With water still high, boys, they ran 'em right by!
Drove them all in the foam where many would die!
And the rest of the herd scattered to the four winds,
and hundreds of cattle were n'ere seen again!

You round up the cattle, keep your night horse with you.
If you're all really lucky it's chuck and quick snooze.
But if the cattle are restless, it's all men to ride.
Keep them circling, and milling, and damn their tough hide!

Then it's back on the trail, boys, at the breakin' of day.
No rest for the weary, we've the devil to pay!
So it's work for short wages, and ride those long hours,
down the Great Western Trail, boys, is no place for cowards!

Great Western, Great Western, you've taken your toll,
still from Texas to Kansas we're rarin' to go!

Through desert and sagebrush and the great tall grass prairie
roll our wagons and cattle - come on, boys, don't tarry!
On to Dodge City, to the end of the trail,
where we'll all get drunk, boys, and raise us some hell!

Great Western, Great Western, the Great Western Trail,
where the best of the cowboys so often have failed.
Where the grit and the grime and the pay's such a pity,
just riding and cussing our way to Dodge City!

Then it's on back to Texas and broke before home!
Forsaking our vow that we'll never more roam,
we sign with a new herd that's headed up North,
and we'll be back on The Western as a matter of course!

Great Western, Great Western, you Great Western trail,
it's the life of a cowboy that you know so well.
It's the riding, and roping, and the wide open plains,
driving cattle from Texas and working for change!

Now the days of the Western, boys, have rolled right on by,
leaving only old memories and cowboys who sigh.
They miss the low of the cattle and the wind and the hail,
and the hard work and ways of the Great Western Trail!

Little Sahara—Photo by Melissa Burns

LITTLE SAHARA

Hot sun beats down, fiery engines roar,
and over dunes they fly!

From far and near they gather to ride the sand
that for miles is rolling high and dry!

It's the Little Sahara, up Watonga way,
and it's a sight to see - sand on sand, wave on wave!

It's here the Dune buggies play, in miles and miles of sand!
They are troubadours of this dusty land -
this roving gypsy band!

Near Medicine Park, OK - Photo by Eddie Wilcoxen

<u>QUIET COVE</u>

The mighty currents of the world's humanity
rush along at a powerful pace!
Famous cities mark the spots
where the strongest currents race.

New York, Paris, London, Tokyo -
they are all in the mainstream,
while others are in a slower flow;
and more easily swum, I deem!

I live in a backwater
of this big old spinning globe,
and the pace is slow and lazy;
it's just a quiet little cove.

I watch the distant waters roar and tear,
and I feel no urge to swim.
From my vantage point of sweet repose,
it looks smooth right where I am.

I enjoy brief forays out
to where the swift white waters run,
but I quickly retreat to my tranquil home
when my adventure's done!

So, if you love the challenge,
Good luck, and steady as she goes!
But as for me, it's the backwater,
and life in a quiet little cove!

FALL SHOW

The wind is rustling in the trees,
it rattles through the leaves
and says, "Get ready! Winter's near!" -
message carried on the breeze.

So, Summer sadly packs her things,
as Autumn proudly shows
those brief, bright colors on a stage of glory
before the coming snows!

BILL PICKETT

Bill Pickett was the "Dusky Bulldog Man", from *The 101* of cowboy fame.
He'd leap on a wild, running steer, bite it's lip and throw him down -
he made himself a name!

He toured the whole world over, putting on a show,
the star of *The 101*! Everywhere Bill Pickett went the crowd would all want more!

They call it steer wrestling now, but it was "Bulldogging" in its day,
because Bill had seen a dog handle a steer that very same, strange way.

Bill was not just a showman; he was a hard working cowboy, too,
and after his retirement, he came back to help *The Miller 101*
with all the things that he could do.

He was killed while busting broncs to help *The 101*;
it took him eleven days to die; there was nothing that could be done.

At his funeral, Will Rogers and Tom Mix, the biggest stars of the day,
said of the cowboy Bill Pickett, there weren't words good enough to say.

And Mr. Miller said Bill was the greatest working cowboy that he had ever seen.
The humble son of former slaves, Bill had lived the American dream!

Respected by every one, and loved by those he knew,
Bill Pickett left a legacy that's matched by very few!

He's in the Professional Rodeo Cowboy's Hall of Fame,
and as long as there is Rodeo, we will honor up his name!

So here's to old Bill Pickett, a true man of the West.
It's said among the cowboys that Bill Pickett was the best!

Photo by Barbara Blocker

SPRING RAIN

It's a quiet Oklahoma morning; angel tears are falling down;
a gentle rain of joyful drops is tumbling to the ground!

And the early spring flowers are rejoicing, they drink with greedy mouth,
so that they in turn, their cheerful blaze can splash out all about!

The land here is awakening from its fitful winter sleep,
and quickens to the pulse of life, and dreams of far off summer's reap.

But first there is work to do, the foundation must be laid.
To prepare for future bounty, we must labor in these days.

So till the land, prepare the seed, the time is near at hand!
Embrace the rain, it's Nature's gain, soon our crops will fill the land!

CATTLE DRIVE

The south end of northbound cows ain't really that exciting;
add in some dust and wind, and the nighttime chill a' biting,

and you've got a cattle drive; herding cattle to the railhead,
rolling North to Kansas, on across the Red!

It's the gateway to the Indian lands where the cattle are well fed.
We graze 'em slow to keep 'em fat, so some money we can make.
At trails end, a different view, as we sit down to eat some steak!

Out there on that trail; whether Chisum, Western or Goodnight;
they sure don't feed you beef - the bosses are just too tight.

It's beans and mesquite coffee, and a little hardtack, too.
It's not all that savory, but it'll see you through.

And it'll make you dream of trail's end and all the comforts there;
women and a warm bed, whiskey, and a place to wash your hair!

It's tough out on the trail, and those cattle seldom rest.
Telling tales when it's all over is the part I like the best!

So I'll ride the night herd, and still be up before the dawn,
cause the quicker we get them moving, the sooner I'll be done!

Oklahoma Longhorns - Photo by Eddie Wilcoxen

LADDER OF RIVERS

Let's get the cattle moving, it's time to travel on.
Put away that harmonica, there's no time for a song!

We've got to climb the Ladder of the Rivers, on our way up to the North.
We move from water to water on our winding rugged course.

In Oklahoma we cross the Red, and then the Washita and more,
up to the Canadian, the Cimarron, and on across the Arkansas.

River to river, rung to rung - get those cattle moving, boys,
cause Kansas here we come!

OKLAHOMA PROUD

It was a spectacle that will never be repeated.
To make the run of '89 a strong constitution was much needed!

Tens of thousands were just milling till that cannon shot split the air,
then the earth exploded in their haste to be the first one there.

It was the lure of land, the currency of kings,
a place to call their very own, the stuff of nearing dreams!

In one day, entire cities sprouted from the earth; Guthrie, Stillwater,
Kingfisher, Oklahoma City, El Reno, Norman, and more;
all were given birth!

By nighttime, April 22, 1889, the Promised Land
was dotted with the campfires of the thousands;
new citizens of a new land, ready to build a life where each can stand.

Stand tall and proud of what we've built!
Stand true and strong and free of guilt!
Stand up and proclaim this Oklahoma land,
a place to live that's truly grand!

SOUTHWEST OKLAHOMA

I've watched the Eagle on the wing, seen the vulture ride the wind,
I've seen the turkey in the draw, heard the coyote his lonely message send.

I've stood atop the mountains and breathed deep of peace and freedom.
I've wandered down her rivers, through her woods, and man, I need 'em!

This rugged, hidden jewel is home to me for thirty years.
In an urban world, it's a quiet refuge, away from city fears!

It's where nature's just around the corner, and friendly people near.
When I think of all I've gained, I shed a happy tear!

BAT CAVE

The curling wisp of smoke isn't what it seems.
It's the rising tide of free-tailed bats taking to the wing!

They pour out in untold thousand to hunt across the skies.
From this place they call the Bat Cave, they fly, and fly and fly!

It's one of the largest nursery caves for the Mexican Free-Tailed Bat,
but it's on private land, and few know where it's at.

Out in Southwest Oklahoma, near the town of Reed,
you can park along the road in summer, and watch them as they leave!

GUSHER

It was raining money, so they say, when a well came in.
That black gold poured down from the sky, and covered all the men.

Gusher was the name they used, and it told the story well.
The bubbling crude would shoot out high, like a freight train up from hell!

The force of the blowout would make machinery twist and groan,
and if a friction spark resulted, it chilled right to the bone!

As fire would erupt from everywhere; the world would be ablaze;
and many a hard working roughneck was laid thus in his grave!

Shooting up two hundred feet or more, the oil would block the clouds,
but despite the dangers of the wild, wild well, the men would shout out loud!

They'd be shaking hands, and clapping backs, and laughing all the while;
they knew a bonus was close at hand, and that they'd go to town in style!

It was always feast or famine out in those Oklahoma fields;
either dry holes or gusher, not much in the way of other deals.

So when that rumble started, way down underground,
it was a time to celebrate! Oil had just been found!

Photo by Barbara Blocker

SEVEN HELLS

It was a time of struggle, out there on this land;
before the wires, before the roads, before there were even wells,

when starry eyed folk, filled with hope,
settled here to build themselves a life,
not knowing of the seven hells.

Number one was drought, often the rains just never came!
And number two was summer heat, parched crops left lying lame.

Number three was winter's cold, that chilled clear to the bone.
Number four was loneliness. No neighbors near -
you were out here all alone!

Number five was death and sickness, for yourself and family.
No doctors near, and from illness you just couldn't flee.

Number six was simply, "Can we get this family by?"
"Do we have food, and clothes, and shelter to keep us warm and dry?"

And number seven was the fear of leaving,
that all the work and sacrifice wouldn't be enough.
Yet every day there were those who left, said it was too damn rough.

On these lands of Oklahoma, the old time settlers trod.
They raised houses and cattle, they learned to till the sod.

They battled drought, and cold, and summer heat,
worried about sickness and getting food to eat.

They hung on to this land with grim determination;
faced hardship beyond belief, more than we can mention.

Today we have all we need and more; we live so very well!
But there was a time when every day,
the people here faced the seven hells.

So just remember where it started, and how it came to be!
Honor them with great respect - they built this Oklahoma land.
We are their legacy!

Cotton Southwest of Altus - Photo by Joan Wilcoxen

Here in Altus, every year we have "Farm/City Week." It's a chance for city and military folks to drive a tractor, and visit various farm operations around the area: cattle, peanuts, cotton, dairy, etc.

There is an annual "Legend of Agriculture Award" for outstanding contributions. In 2006 it went to the Boll Weevil Eradication Program. It was well deserved!

Before they started the eradication program, cotton acreage and yield was dropping dramatically. When they started, in the late 90's they were trapping thousands of weevils per acre. This current year, there have been no weevils caught, and production and profits have soared.

When I found out I was going to get to make this presentation at the banquet, I just had to write this poem.

--------------Eddie D. Wilcoxen

KING COTTON

Old King Cotton was all tuckered out,
And all he could do was just moan and shout!

Where had all of those good times gone?
How in the world did it get so wrong?

Once there was cotton, far as the eye could see.
Now, no white fields in sight, he thought, "Oh, woe is me!"

"It's that bug, that blasted weevil!
I swear to you that boy is evil!

We plant a crop, try to make some money,
then he shows up, and it ain't funny!

He has more relatives than a dog has fleas,
and they just help themselves to what they please!

I guess it's over, my day is done.
It's the end of cotton, them dang bugs have won!"

Yes, Old King Cotton was ready to quit!
Just throw in the towel, give in to the hit!

When, suddenly on the horizon appeared
some knights in white armor who said, "Please Don't Fear!"

"We have come from afar to help you out here!
We're the Boll Weevil Slayers - you've nothing to fear!"

"So, please don't you worry, we're here to win!
Gonna take out that weevil and all of his kin!"

They said, "Fear not, old King, for now we are here!
And vigilant and watchful, we keep our potions near!

We seek the dreaded weevil, wherever he may be,
and we fight and we win, and keep us all pest free!

Why, we fly through the air and magic potions we drop!
They choke out that mad bug - we'll save this here crop!"

Soon Old King Cotton could not believe his eyes.
In just a few short years, the cotton piled high!

The farmers rejoiced and the King was re-crowned.
They held a big ball - a party renowned!

And the knights were the heroes - all applauded their dedication,
And raised cups to the brave lads of Boll Weevil Eradication!

Yes, Boll Weevil Eradication, like the heroes of old,
saved the day for us all - now their story's been told.

And so all lived forever happy in that Oklahoma land,
and this legend tells the tale of that merry little band!

OKLAHOMA LULLABY

I hear the night wind sighing, the cottonwood's soft creak,
and I look to find you sleeping, and gently kiss your cheek.

Goodnight, my child, goodnight; may your dreams be long and sweet.
May morning find you rested, and ready to run and play on dancing feet!

From my porch I hear the far off cry of coyotes, as the crickets chirp nearby,
while I sit here rocking quietly in this Oklahoma lullaby!

Haystack Mountain - Photo by Joan Wilcoxen

TURNER FALLS

Turner Falls in the moonlight is a most romantic sight:
the surrounding trees, the mountain road,
the shimmering silvery light!

There's the sound of falling waters and shadows in the night;
they make it quite mysterious, the realm of water sprites.

You can walk here through the woodlands, down the moonlit path,
and sit and watch the waters fall, until you wander back.

In the day, the people rush, the children splash and shout,
but in the quiet night, only the night birds are about.

I've sat alone besides these waters and I've been here hand in hand.
Turner Falls is lovely either way.

But Turner Falls in the moonlight with someone you love,
is a romantic, sweet bouquet!

Turner Falls - Photo by Barbara Blocker

THE '89ERS

Hear the thunder of the hoof beats, feel excitement in the air!
There's land here for the taking, so ride hard without a care!

In carts and wagons, horseback and afoot, the thronging multitude stands ready,
waiting for the gunshot that will start this famous run.

They are the '89ers - Oklahoma's proud wild sons!

Hell bent for land, they raced across this rugged prairie scene,
to start a life and build a state, to hold in hand a dream -

a dream of something better, a dream of hearth and home;
built from blood, and sweat, and love, of dirt and sticks and stone.

These were fiercely independent folks, ready to risk it all,
for just a chance at Oklahoma land. They'd heard the siren call!

The dream of America: "Own your own," it said!
"Ride hard in the land rush and to the land be wed.

Here you can raise your children, teach them to love the land,
show them how to live life right, to believe and make a stand."

And someday, there'll be roads and bridges, towns and trains, and places you can dine,
but right now it's only empty land, waiting for the coming tide to ride in 1889!

EAGLE WATCH

The soaring eagle sails aloft with a crown of snowy white!
He rolls and wheels across the sky behind the mountain's height.

He reappears, joined by another, and together they ride the wind!
It's winter at Quartz Mountain, and the eagles are back again!

Each year when the Northlands shiver, the eagles here return;
they come to Oklahoma, where winter is less stern.

They fish these placid waters, and sit upon the rocks.
They ride the rising thermals; it's here the eagles flock!

It's winter at Quartz Mountain and excitement's running high.
We scan the skies with eager eyes as the eagles soar on by!

Quartz Mountain Lugert Altus Dam - Photo by Nelda Cable

QUARTZ MOUNTAINS

Have you ever seen the Quartz Mountains shining in the sun,
their granite faces sparkling with the gems for which they're known?

Have you ever seen the morning mist hide the rocky tops,
or seen the flash of deer, or the gobbling turkey flocks?

Have you ever seen the climbers on Mighty Baldie's soaring slab?
They come from near and far here, to give the best they have!

Have you seen the soaring eagle, and the vulture and the hawk?
These mighty birds of prey circle high, and hunt among the rocks.

Have you ever seen a gentle rain tumble down the mountain side,
growing swiftly to a torrent, seeking out the river's ride?

Have you ever seen the colors that the fall can bring,
like God just took a giant brush and swept over everything?

The golds, the reds, the falling leaves - it's really quite a show!
And it's hidden here in the Old Southwest, a place that few folks know!

I've seen these old Quartz Mountains in sunshine, fog, and rain.
I've climbed to hidden valleys, and I hope I will again.

I've seen the sights of all the world, cause I've been known to roam,
and I've enjoyed them all, but there still no place like home!

So when I see these old Quartz Mountains it brings to me relief,
and says, "My boy, you're nearing home, with its sweet and gentle peace!"

Jim Thorpe was one of the most amazing athletes of the twentieth century, and a personal hero of mine. Of Sac and Fox and Irish mixed heritage, Jim Thorpe's given name was Wa-Tho-Huk, meaning, "Bright Path", and his athletic skill was truly phenomenal.

In the 1912 Stockholm Olympics he won both the decathlon and the pentathlon and was declared by the host King of Sweden as "The World's Greatest Athlete!"

He went on to play professional baseball, professional basketball, and professional football. In fact, he was the first player inducted into the Pro Football Hall of Fame.
.......Eddie D. Wilcoxen

JIM THORPE

Jim Thorpe, Bright Path, famous running man!
Oklahoma's own, greatest athlete in this land!

At the 1912 Olympics he was named the world's best,
and the King of Sweden pinned the medal on his chest.

Then they stripped him of his honors for a wrong he never knew.
It wasn't just the loss of medals - they called him a cheater -
hurt him through and through!

And all those long years later, after Jim was dead and gone,
they said it was all a mistake, that they had done him wrong.

I know somewhere Jim Thorpe could hear, and cried himself a tear,
to know the honor of his name was back, to echo through the years.

Jim Thorpe, the Oklahoma Indian, was the greatest in the land!
Jim Thorpe, Bright Path, famous running man!

Photo by Eddie Wilcoxen

POND SONG

Above my pond, a summer song
is sung so sweet and clear.
A dragonfly is flitting by,
while butterflies linger near.

Nearby the crickets chirp and work;
they rest here in the grass.
And frogs will join the chorus
when day is mostly past.

The music of the water's splash
is the base note for it all -
the drumming beat, the swift repeat
of waters as they fall.

While below and lazing slow,
the goldfish wander on.
And in the trees a chickadee
bursts out in happy song!

And in my heart a gladness starts,
to enjoy such interplay,
as above my pond, a summer song
is heard most every day!

Forest Path in the Wichita Mountains - Photo by Eddie Wilcoxen

FOREST MAGIC

A forest trail, a distant waterfall,
the majestic mountains rise around me.
And I feel nature call, saying, "Come and look!
Come find your peace! Come see the wonder of it all!"

It's the rippling of a stream,
soft burbling of a brook,
gentle sounds soft in the forest,
that call for you to look,
and to sit awhile beside the flowing water.

Enjoy life without the hassle,
as the light filters through the trees in shafts of
golden magic, like columns in a fairy castle!

And all around the song of birds
fills your heart with joy,
as the pain of the years melts away,
and once again you are a boy.

Fresh and innocent, young and wild,
looking at life through the eyes of a child!
Here in the forest, these things really happen.
Just rest and unwind, and let your mind run wild!

SCISSORTAIL

Out in the Oklahoma prairie, away from bustling towns,
if you look to the skies and wires, a special bird is found.

It's the state bird, the scissortail, so well and aptly named;
the long feathers and split tail is how he gained his fame.

A roving flycatcher, the scissortail in flight
dips and darts and swoops; it's really quite a sight!

And when at rest, his beauty can be seen.
No better choice for our state bird, could any ever dream!

THE THREE GUARDSMEN

There are some names from Oklahoma's past that you should really know.
And on any list of one time greats, there are three that always show.

The "Three Guardsmen" were U.S. Deputies in the Indian Territory.
The outlaws gave them that name, and helped spread their tale of glory!

Heck Thomas, Bill Tilghman, and Chris Madden
rode the Oklahoma Hills and trails,
and they captured hundreds of desperadoes and took them off to jail.

They were considered smart, and strong, and true, by everyone around.
They helped to build a new land, and to finally calm things down.

Heck Thomas went on to be a sheriff. He moved off to Lawton,
and when discussing the Doolins or the Daltons his name will come up often.

Bill Tilghman tried to retire and live a quiet life,
but he was called back into service to quell some oil town strife.

He was gunned down on the streets of Cromwell in 1924,
and soon after Cromwell burned, every house and store!

They say that Chris Madden and his lawman friends
were the ones to strike the match,
but no charges were ever made; no one even asked.

Chris Madden lived until 1944, he died at 93.
With him passed the last of these men who lived life wild and free.

They were called the "Three Guardsmen"; may their names live on in fame.
They brought law to this Oklahoma territory - their like won't come again!

THE HANGING JUDGE
(JUDGE PARKER)

The gallows cast a forlorn shadow across a troubled land,
where the hanging judge, Isaac Parker, ruled with a stern and mighty hand.

His was the court of no appeal, his decision was the law,
and dozens hung at his decree, filled the outlaw class with awe!

He made law from Fort Smith, Arkansas, but his domain was the Indian Territory.
When he ascended to the bench in 1875 he began a western story.

At his first term in court, he sentenced eight to die.
He commuted one, another shot; that left six to be hung high.

And on that fateful day; it was on down in the fall;
hundreds there were gathered, before the prison walls.

Six death warrants were read aloud, then six men climbed the scaffold.
Then the levers pulled, and six men fell, swinging dead and cold!

It was the first law in the territory, and it was swift and rough,
but the honest folks were grateful; they'd lived in fear enough.

In twenty years Judge Parker made his legend on the Oklahoma bench;
he hung all of eighty eight, and brought law and order before his time was spent!

COMING HOME

Tonight I'm thinking about my Oklahoma home;
I've been away too long!
Far out over the Pacific, I'm looking home,
and in my heart a song!

A tune of the old southwest,
of the mountains and the plain;
of people helping people, giving respect,
and getting back the same!

And I'm thinking about the prairie
and that wide old open sky,
and I'm ready to be there -
 ready to see the cattle graze, and watch the eagle fly.

It's been fun to travel, good to see the world,
but it's great to be back home, where the pace of life is slow.
So I'm going to light a fire, relax and put my feet up,
and wander nevermore!

Photo by Cheri Maloney

BRAHMA LESSON

Those boys out at the rodeo have sure got my respect;
before I'd sit a Brahma Bull, I'd take an old car wreck!

At least in the case of crashing cars, I can belt myself down tight,
but when those big old bulls unwind, you might just die of fright!

A toss or two of snorting mad and horned bull ain't my style,
so I'll just stand and watch them go and cheer them all the while.

Because even though I'll never ride a bull, and I'll never ever try,
it's a thrill and a sight to see! Who knew that man can really fly?

Then sometimes a cowboy gets it right and finds that old sweet spot.
He stays aboard with style and grace and gives it all he's got!

In that moment it's both art and strength at play,
and reminds you that special things can be done by those who stay!

Keep on trying, keep on getting up, get right back up on the problem.
Learn a lesson from the cowboy; ride for all you're worth!
And soon enough you've solved 'em!

Wichitas - Photo by Eddie Wilcoxen

Near our house in southwest Oklahoma are some of the most ancient mountains in the world. The Wichita Mountains were around with the ancestral Rockies, which have been worn down, and have risen again.

The Wichitas were once as high above the surrounding terrain as the modern Rockies, but now, with the passing of eons they have filled the valleys and worn their peaks until all that remains is an amazing backbone of ancient granite and surrounding prairie, encompassed within the Wichita Mountains National Wildlife Preserve.

............*Eddie D. Wilcoxen*

THE WICHITAS

These rocky craggy peaks surprise the retreating plain.
Ancient jumbled boulders thrust
and push their way upon the scene.

The grasslands crash upon unbroken rock
and fall away dissatisfied, as if the stone does mock
their domain and their right to cover all,
except the soaring hawk.

Granite boulders pile high under summer sun and heat,
forbidding and foreboding, yet drawing you to seek
some ancient tie, some connection to the past -
a sense of things you ought to know -
of mysteries revealed at last.

Long down these paths have traveled,
and in these rocks have battled,
the Indians of America;
hear the echo of their plaintive cry,
and the creak of the cowboy's saddle!

Caddo, Comanche, Kiowa, Apache;
all sought their solace here.
With its bounty rich and shelter warm,
the Wichitas were winter home.
No blizzards here to fear!

The Wichitas of Oklahoma -
still home of the wild and the free -
a place to hike and look and learn
or just to merely "be."
Here vast herds of buffalo still wander,
with deer, and elk, and longhorn,
and playful prairie dogs to ponder!

Stretching mile on mile,
it's a rugged land unending,
filled with beauty, yes,
but ruled by nature's laws unbending.

An ancient rocky fortress
that guards the past and keeps it close at hand,
the Wichitas are yours to roam -
a glimpse beyond the pavement
at America's wild land!

SEQUOYAH

The written word has strength, it carries with it power,
and those that possess it are ensconced in Ivory Towers!

Sequoyah was a Cherokee, raised in the tribal ways,
and he marveled at the white man's words, written down and saved.

He knew the Cherokee deserved this skill, and he began to work.
For a dozen years he planned and tried, went from warrior to a clerk.

And there were many hardships; he was ridiculed and scorned,
many believed him crazy or to the devil born.

But Sequoyah believed the "talking leaves" for his tribe were very near,
and ignoring all the tumult, he tried and persevered!.

He is the only man in history to by himself create an alphabet,
and with this invention all Cherokee were in his debt.

He showed the tribal leaders, demonstrated it for them,
and they praised him for his wisdom, said "teach it to our kin!"

Within months, there were many would could write in Cherokee,
and thanks to Sequoyah, many teachings were preserved for history.

In 1828 the Cherokee Phoenix was in print for all to read,
the first ever Indian Newspaper, it was the starting seed.

The Cherokee were already great, and in that we can rejoice,
but Sequoyah's alphabet unified a people,
and gave that people voice!

JESTER'S CAVE

Long ago they took me to Jester's Cave; traveling
northwest of Mangum, Oklahoma, a winding path we made.

Until at last, back in the Gypsum hills a yawning cavern showed,
and they said, "This is Jester's Cave, a place of legends bold!"

It meanders just underground, for miles back in these hills,
and just inside the entrance, and to the right is quite a thrill!

It's a tunnel that angles ten feet down, with a small room at the end.
It was dug by someone who came here back in the 30's and quickly left again.

No one knows just who he was or from whence he came.
Some said California, said he had a treasure map, and didn't give his name.

He dug at Jester's Cave for weeks, you can still see the iron tracks,
where with a mining car he'd haul out the dirt he dug with pick and ax.

They say that he left happy, never told what he had found,
but he stopped for gas in Mangum, and word soon got around.

In the back of his car, right there on the seat,
were three rusted guns, and something wrapped and tucked up underneath.

When they asked him what he'd found, he just said, "Enough!"
and left everyone to wonder just what all it was.

Now we'll never know, it was just too long ago,
but Jester's Cave is still up there - take me with you if you go!

Old Saddle Mountain School near Cutthroat Gap - Photo by Joan Wilcoxen

CUTTHROAT GAP

In the upper reaches of the Wichitas is a place called Cutthroat Gap.
When you come to Oklahoma, you'll find it right there on the map.

It gets its name from true events back in 1833,
when the Osage attacked the Kiowa and massacred all who couldn't flee.

There was a band of Kiowa camped here, mostly woman, old and children.
The warriors had gone to gather horses and then on North to raid again.

On a quiet summer morning, the Osage flew down from the rocks,
and with long knives and grim faces, they began to make their mark.

Many Kiowa escaped that day; they lived to tell the tale,
but none forgot the horror when they returned to that lonely dale.

Scattered all around were the missing of their kin -one hundred fifty strong -
their heads removed and in cooking pots, the bodies on the ground!

The Kiowa never again camped out on this plain because
they say on summer nights to this place those departed spirits came!

For almost a hundred years in spring, on one night of the year,
a Kiowa would climb a nearby mountain to sing and pray for spirits lingering near.

That's why they call it Cutthroat Gap; the story has been told.
It was before the coming of the White Man, in the Warrior Days of old!

SPANISH SILVER

The lure of gold and silver, the riches from the earth,
drew the Spanish long ago to their Oklahoma search.

The legends say the Spaniards from far off Santa Fe
found silver in the Devil's Canyon, and mined it straight away.

High up in the hills of the Quartz Mountains, the Spaniards dug and dug -
but just where still isn't known - time's secret still kept smug.

There are stories told of glimpses of treasure troves and maps,
and if you want a story told, you only have to ask!

But no one really knows how much, or if silver was ever found.
But we do know the Spanish came here many times,
and dug in this Oklahoma ground!

Quanah Parker - Photo Courtesy Museum of the Western Prairie, Altus, OK

QUANAH PARKER

Quanah Parker, Quahada Warrior, stepped across the ages,
with one foot in a storied past, the other in modern history's pages!

The son of Chief Nocona, a Comanche through and through,
Quanah battled across the western plains - many times he counted coup!

The Quahada refused the reservation way,
said, "We were born free men, and free men we will stay!"

They raided and they fought all along the old frontier,
and the very name of Quanah Parker filled the settlers with fear!

At the Battle of Adobe Walls in Texas, 1874,
Quanah was badly wounded and almost found the other shore.

But finally the time of change had come. In 1875,
Quanah sought a vision and saw an eagle fly.

The eagle turned its wings and flew off toward Fort Sill,
then Quanah saw a wolf alone high atop a hill.

He knew the days of the Comanche would be forever changed,
so he surrendered to the soldiers. Still a great chief he remained.

He helped to guide his people into a changing time,
while holding to their customs as this new world was defined.

He owned part of a railroad, learned the white man's tongue,
negotiated for grazing rights - his interests were far flung.

He was friend of the cowman Goodnight, and President Roosevelt, too,
and he tried his best to guide the Comanche through these days so new.

He kept the peyote habit, and all his wives as well.
When told to send all but one away, he said, "You be the one to tell!"

Quanah Parker, Quahada Warrior, lived and died Comanche style.
Born into the old ways, this modern man showed integrity and courage,
every step of every mile!

BRICKTOWN

A once proud part of a growing city fell into disrepair,
and as time went by the businesses closed, not much going there.

And then this city looked toward the future with an eye aimed at the past,
and realized that these empty buildings had truly been built to last.

So they created themselves a district with a visionary dream,
and called the whole thing, "Bricktown," and set out to make it gleam!

First there was one restaurant, and then a club or two.
But soon there were twenty more and many things to do!

The restored the old canal, built a River Walk so fine,
where floating down the waters amidst sparkling lights is just divine!

They built the Bricktown Baseball Park, no finer to be found,
and movies, shops, and Bass Pro, and the biggest bar around!

And people come from everywhere to enjoy a good time here.
They come to play in "Bricktown," to dance, and dine and cheer!

BRICKTOWN! It's an Oklahoma City of vision and hard work,
and here's a salute to all who dreamed, and laid the solid groundwork!

STATE FAIR

It's cotton candy, corn dogs, and funnel cakes to eat!
It's a crowd along the midway, it's a show that can't be beat!

It's hot tubs for sale, plus tractors, sheds and more.
It's the Ginsu knife demo, and animals by the score.

Horses, pigs, goats and chicks, rabbits, geese and ducks,
cattle of all descriptions, and children run amuck!

It's thousands of people, roaming all around,
looking at exhibitions, some from their own home town.

It's flower shows, race cars, country stoves, and merchants everywhere,
offering strange things for show, and stranger things to wear.

Day after day the people come, like a rushing stream,
and you'll have to see it personally to know just what I mean!

So as the days grow cooler and the nights get longer too,
we'll see you at the State Fair! We'll save a place for you!

Photo by Barbara Blocker

SUNSET OF THE WEST

Self reliant, proud and free, out to make it on his own,
the Western Man made his stand, and built himself a home.

Hauling water, chopping wood, hard work that must be done -
it was the order of the day - chores to do, come rain, or in the blazing sun.

But there was the friendship of honest folks who respected all and one,
and there was laughter, love, and a little time for fun.

Eye to eye and toe to toe, each man his own king,
the Western pioneer made independence ring!

Now the water's from the tap, the wood replaced by gas,
and convention sets the tone; don't do it unless you ask.

Hard work too often is held in disdain, only fit for fools,
and too many men can't fix anything; don't know how to use a tool!

They're city soft and sophisticated, and feel they are smarter,
but they wouldn't last two weeks amidst the hardships where it started!

It's time to recognize the virtues of hard work and honest toil.
It's time to tip our hats to the ranchers and the tillers of the soil.

It's time to know that America grew great by those of a like mind;
who stood up proud, and instead of complaint, embraced the daily grind!

OLD TIMERS

The creak of the wagon passing by,
the daring of the horsemen as they fly;
it seems another world!

But there are those who remember still
the coming of the rail and wheel;
they saw an age unfurl!

With one foot in a rugged past,
they've seen the coming of the car and plane.
In their lifetime TV, A/C, and the Internet all came.

They've seen more changes
than any since the world began,
so let's remember, and give these folks a hand!

Seek them in their quiet places while there yet is time,
and listen to their tales and stories.
To ignore this precious heritage would surely be a crime!

TULSA

Take me back to Tulsa, it's a very old refrain.
Take me back to Tulsa, there's magic in the name!

Take me back to the hills of home, to the friendly people there -
to the smiling faces and helping hands, to a place without a care.

Take me back to the wooded parks, the well kept neighborhoods,
and to the bustling downtown shopping. I'd be there if I could!

And though I'm far away, I see the Arkansas roll by,
and remember fishing in her waters when I wasn't four feet high.

I know that someday I'll return, and then we'll never part,
but until then, Tulsa is a feeling I always carry in my heart!

OKLAHOMA WILDFLOWERS

Across the rugged granite peaks, in the springtime of the year,
bloom Oklahoma wildflowers, reaching far and near.

Hardened rock flanked by the flowers nestled all around,
makes an amazing sight that stretches across the jagged ground.

The colored petals of every hue turn their heads to greet the warming sun,
and gather in appreciation where the springtime rivulets run.

They bask in this brief season of wetness, in the semi arid West,
and roll out a rainbow raiment; they wear only nature's best!

The orange of the Indian Blanket illuminates the hills,
and the sweet vessel of the Wine Cups looks to be by fairies filled.

The golden yellow of the coreopsis, sunflower, and the goldenrod,
rolls on for untold miles,
while scattered asters, bee plants and coneflowers elicit smile on smile.

You can hike through springtime splendor, or just park along the road.
Either way, it's Nature's glory, an Oklahoma story, waiting to be told!

CROSSTIMBERS

A snarl of brush and branches through which you could not make your way,
covered much of Central Oklahoma, way back in the day!

Early explorers traveled miles and miles in order to go around,
because if you entered the Crosstimbers, you might never again be found!

The Crosstimber forest was old beyond its looks,
the trees were not giant but the had the strength it took,

to survive for many hundreds, years piled upon the years,
and the jumble of the branches made this a place to be much feared!

In the early 1800's when Washington Irving tried to pass,
he said this forest is a vexation and seems made of iron cast!

In Oklahoma's craggy reaches the Crosstimbers still gently sleep,
undisturbed by plows and foresters, in country still too tough to reach.

Only a shadow of its former self, in depth and breadth and size,
across Central Oklahoma, the remnants of the great Crosstimbers lie!

HAPPY BIRTHDAY, OKLAHOMA!

Oklahoma! Happy Birthday! Now you are 100 years of age,
leaving adolescence to step upon the world's great stage!

Still young, and fresh and vibrant, with that Pioneer Spirit!
It may not be Heaven, son, but it's mighty near it!

Proud Indian heritage - more than any other place!
Destined for the stars - more Astronauts into outer space!

Scarred by the bombing, joined together by our faith,
always ready with a helping hand, it's a state of grace!

Oklahoma! wedded to the land!
Oklahoma! Proud American stand!
Come and visit, catch the spirit, Oklahoma's grand!

FREEDOM, OKLAHOMA

The hills, the river, and the gypsum rock
near Freedom, roll on mile on mile.

It's ranch country, like an old time Western movie,
and Alabaster Caverns to explore for just a while.

You should get on a horse and ride across
this unspoiled piece of the West.

Then you'll have some small idea of
why we say it is the best!

SPACE SHUTTLE

In the far southwest of Oklahoma
is Altus Air Force Base.

And sometimes it's a stopping place
when the shuttle returns from outer space.

It makes quite a contrast,
prairie views and spaceships!

It reminds us all of how small the world,
and of how the changes quickly shift!

Space Shuttle at Altus Air Force Base— Photo by Paul McEndree

SPACEPORT

And while we're talking spaceships,
don't forget Burns Flat,
where the Oklahoma Spaceport
has tomorrow coming fast!

Suborbital flights are nearing,
and soon we will be flying high,
to kiss the face of the heavens
in this Oklahoma sky!

STRIPERS!
(ODE TO LAKE TEXOMA)

The stripers run in Texoma! What a fishing treat!
Catch Lake Texoma at the right time, and this just can't be beat!

Imported from the ocean to the Red River's salty run,
the Striped Bass grow to fifty pounds; catching them is fun!

And when the stripers are running and chasing fleeing shad,
just cast upon the boiling water, and another fish you'll have!

They're in a feeding frenzy, and eat anything that moves,
and fishermen dream of being in the right place, at this right time, too!

Follow the gulls! They know! They are hunting too,
feeding on the frenzied shad that the stripers herd on through.

It's a conflagration of men, and fish, and birds.
Out on Lake Texoma, it's a sight to be both seen and heard!

When the Lake Texoma stripers hunt and feed among the shad,
you'll find the greatest fishing here that you have ever had!

REMINGTON PARK

The horses race at Remington, in Oklahoma City.
To miss the music of their movement would surely be a pity!

Bred to run and born for speed, around the track they fly,
and images of Winged Pegasus echo as they come thundering by.

Upon their backs the jockeys ride, feet in stirrups high,
and urge them on to greater speed, as their wondrous trade they ply!

Swift and sure footed steeds, their muscles ripple as they run,
and you find yourself pumping in your seat, to the rhythm that they drum!

Lean in and out, and in and out, as if you can change their pace,
and when the race at last is run, relax and check your fate!

Did you win, or did you lose? No matter at this time!
For there are races still to run, and the horses are sublime!

BUFFALOES RETURN

Across these lands, since time was born, strode the mighty buffalo!
But with the white man's guns a booming, soon they all would go!

No more the thundering sound of hooves, in numbers like the blades of grass.
No more the shaggy beasts in herds that took days and days to pass.

They had gone from teaming millions, to a handful in a blink,
and the days and ways of the warrior tribes teetered on the brink.

Without their sustenance, this creature who provided all,
like robes, and food, and rawhide ropes, the tribal ways must fall!

When the buffalo were gone, the plains Indians were removed.
With their mobile larder gone, to fight on would be no use!

They moved on to reservations, and dreamt of bygone days,
before the changing times had stripped away their ancient ways.

And then one day a rumor swept across Fort Sill,
that the buffalo were returning to graze these rocky hills!

The Wichita Mountain Wildlife Refuge would hold them once again,
and here the buffalo would roam as had ever been.

When the Indians of the area heard the long sought news,
some walked more than twenty miles just to get a view.

Whole families walked and walked; they traveled through the night
just to be on hand when the train pulled into sight.

For the buffalo was more than food, more than clothing, too.
It was a symbol of the way of life that they both loved and knew!

They danced and sang and prayed for days, sending grateful thanks in smoke.
They came to see these wondrous creatures - the buffaloes -
through which the Great Spirit always spoke.

Wichita Mountains Wildlife Refuge Buffalo - Photo by Tyrone Penick

MEDICINE PARK

Medicine Park, a place of Indian power,
Oklahoma's first resort, with rising granite towers.

Where the water slowly meanders, and happy people play.
It's a great place to visit, and a better place to stay!

Gateway to the Wichitas, an artist colony in the rock,
with nature's beauty gleaming; a place to escape the rigors of the clock.

Mount Scott rises in the west, with Lake Lawtonka in between.
Come and enjoy historic Medicine Park, quiet and pristine!

DEATH SONG

A slight old man, not big at all, was shuffling to the wagon,
weighed down by iron that bound his hands, and by the chains that he was draggin'.

Softly he sang as he onward came, noticed by very few,
but one lone trooper came to his guard to tell them what to do.

"You better watch that one," he said, "He's spoiling for a fight;
that chant you hear is his death song, so be careful on the ride."

But they were many and he was one - just an old and scrawny man,
so they laughed and said, "Don't worry, we've got things well in hand."

There were six guards in the wagon, with the handcuffed man within,
and as they left Fort Sill, they joked, and talked of places they had been.

On the road to Fort Reno, the old man uttered not one sound,
but behind his back he worked the metal cuffs as against his skin he ground.

He cut himself clean to the bone, and never showed a sign,
and with the blood for lubrication, quietly pulled one hand aside.

Then suddenly as a hunting cat, he struck without a clue,
swinging the handcuffs, he hit one man, knocked his weapon loose.

Instantly, he grabbed the gun and another trooper ate the stock,
and as he fell the others stood frozen, victims of the shock!

The Indian fired and shot them all, then turned his attention south,
to the mounted soldiers riding behind upon their Calvary mounts.

He fired once, and the rifle jammed, so the old man changed his plans,
and leaping from the wagon, straight at the troopers ran!

Twenty guns exploded, and one old man fell dead,
but not before his song was sung, and his heart to bravery wed!

KILL THE MOUNTAIN

In old time Oklahoma, here's a story that they tell,
of the man who killed a mountain, and all the wealth it held.

Near present day Snyder was a massive mountain of black rock,
the finest granite ever, the pride of miner's talk.

It was owned by a man in Russia, who never seemed to pay
the hard working Oklahoman who toiled his days away.

Finally the man from Snyder sent a letter out -
it said, "Pay me what you owe me, or I'll smash the mountain down!"

Oh, how the Russian chuckled, and sent back this reply,
"No doubt you're a mighty man but that mountain's mighty high!
You do what you feel you have to do, but don't you threaten me.
I'll hire another quarry man, and not one cent you'll see!"

So, the man set about to work; he was an expert at his craft;
he planted explosives all around, though some said he was daft!

When he set off the charges, the mountain didn't fall,
but every grain of granite fractured as with a giant's maul!

In one smashing moment, he killed the mountain dead,
and I've often wondered what thoughts went through his head!

Though still standing, the rock had been destroyed.
Not a slab was left undamaged, no black granite to be enjoyed!

Then the man left for parts unknown, and was never seen again,
and not one more piece was ever quarried—some said it was a sin!

Like the old rock man who told this tale to me.
He said that old black granite was the finest that you would ever see!

But it's ruined now, killed by spite and greed,
and buried under water in the depths of Lake Tom Steed!

ROLLIN' HOME

I rolled North into Oklahoma past that old Red River flood.
Glad to be back home, here in the land of living good.

You'll have to forgive my pleasure, and perhaps you'll forgive my pride,
but nothing beats these Oklahoma skies!

The people here are friendly, the people here are best.
They'll make you understand about hospitality in the West!

So my heart always quickens, I always feel a thrill,
when at the end of my road, I see those Oklahoma hills!

Our home in southwest Oklahoma - Photo by Eddie Wilcoxen

SO GLAD I'M HOME

Steam rising from a coffee cup -
quiet time, no one else is up.
So glad I'm home.

I've been traveling way too far -
by airplane, taxi and by car.
So glad I'm home.

Living day to day -
way too far away, I just got to say,
So glad I'm home.

Home, home, where your love light shines.
Home, with your hand in mine.
Home, where I'll stay this time.
Darling, help me sing this line -
So glad I'm home!

Tired of staying at the Motel 6.
Worn out from all these business trips,
and from playing all their fancy tricks.
So glad I'm home!

Darlin', let's turn out the light.
Let me hold you in the night.
Hold you close, and oh, so tight!
So glad I'm home!

Home, home, where your love light shines,
Home, with your hand in mine.
Home, where I'll stay this time.
Darling, help me sing this line -
So glad I'm home!

OKLAHOMA CITY MEMORIAL

In Oklahoma City terror struck - there's no defense for madness!
In the aftermath, emotions boiled. There was anger - there was sadness.

The who, the why, the questions, spinning in each head,
as the torn and shattered building fell around the many dead.

Crisis is the crucible where character is forged and found,
and the people of Oklahoma stood tall and held their ground.

They put aside their tears and did the work they had to face,
and felt the soothing comfort of a nation's warm embrace.

From all across America, the prayers and people poured,
to help in Oklahoma - to help beat back the sword.

A handful of ignorant and evil men wreaked havoc in OKC,
but in the end, grace and goodness triumphed over death's decree!

Today there is a memorial where the Murrah Building stood,
a place to mourn the fallen, to remember all things good.

It's a monument to courage, and to the strength of love,
a place where people go to reflect and send prayers to up above!

Oklahoma City Memorial - Photos by Nelda Cable

HOME

Home, a place where I belong.
It's where they know my name, and where I get along!

It's where I'm accepted for what and who I am.
It's where there are friends to help me if I get in a jam.

A man could search the world, could forever roam,
and somehow miss the mark—never find a home!

Here I know I have those who remember me, and I remember them,
a connection to a place and time worth more to me than gems!

Home and not alone! What a blessing to receive!
A feeling so warm and good it's hard to quite believe!

Home is where the heart is, and mine beats within my chest,
in perfect time to the rhythm of this one place, I know it suits me best!

OKLAHOMA PROUD! INDEX

Acknowledgements, 7

Bat Cave, 60
Beaver's Bend, 30
Belle Starr, 36
Bill Pickett, 56
Black Mesa, 23
Brahma Lesson, 79
Bricktown, 88
Buckskin Joe, 28
Buffaloes Return, 98

Cattle Drive, 58
Cheshire Moon, 49
Coming Home, 78
Coyotes, 45
Crosstimbers, 93
Cutthroat Gap, 84

Death Song, 100

Eagle Watch, 70

Fall Show, 55
Forest Magic, 74
Fox, 45
Freedom, Oklahoma, 94

Geronimo, 39
Goodbye to the Cowboy, 35
Great Western Trail, 51
Gusher!, 61
Guthrie, 37

Happy Birthday, Okalahoma!, 94
Heavener Runestone, 38
Home, 105
Hugo Bluegrass, 16

Introduction, 8

Jester's Cave, 83
Jim Thorpe, 72
Jumping the Cimarron, 32

Kill the Mountain, 101
King Cotton, 65

Ladder of Rivers, 59
Lights in the Valley Tonight, 25
Little Prairie Home, 26
Little Sahara, 53

Medicine Park, 99
Mistletoe, 22

Oil!, 18
Oklahoma City Memorial, 104
Oklahoma Difference, 44
Oklahoma Home, 40
Oklahoma Lullaby, 67
Oklahoma Proud!, 59
Oklahoma Wildflowers, 100
Old Timers, 91

Pond Song, 73
Price Falls, 20

Quanah Parker, 87
Quartz Mountains, 71
Quiet Cove, 54

Rattlesnakes, 41
Red River Sunset, 48
Redbud, 17
Remington Park, 97
Rhyming the Western Sky, 11
Rollin' Home, 102
Route 66, 12

OKLAHOMA PROUD! INDEX
(continued)

Scissortail, 75
Sequoyah, 82
Seven Hells, 62
So Glad I'm Home, 103
Sooner, Not Later, 33
Southwest Oklahoma, 60
Space Shuttle, 95
Spaceport, 95
Spanish Silver, 85
Spring Rain, 57
Stand Waite, 24
State Fair, 89
Stripers (Ode to Lake Texoma), 96
Sunset of the West, 90

Thanks Theodore, 14
The 89'ers, 69
The Hanging Judge, 77
The Three Guardsmen, 76
The Wichitas, 80
Thunderstorm, 42
Tulsa, 91
Turner Falls, 68

Wiley Post, 47
Will Rogers, 46
Winter, 31

CTK PUBLISHING

Thanks for spending some time with <u>Oklahoma Proud!</u>

Please visit our website **Eddiestuff.com**

It has the latest information on the current projects. There is also a place to click to wander through our garden!

Here is a list of poetry books that I have written, which are either published or in the process of being made available:

- **Reflections of a Wandering Mind**
- **More Reflections of a Wandering Mind**
- **Still Reflecting!**
- **Songbook in My Head**
- **Songs from the Heart**
- **Oklahoma Proud!**
- **Train of Thought**
- **ABC's of Whimsy**

Once more, thank you! Until we get together again, "Take care, and take the time to be good to somebody!"

…………..Eddie D. Wilcoxen